RUNNING FOR DAYBREAK

RUNNING FOR DAYBREAK

Poems

Richard Alan Bunch

Mellen Poetry Press
Lewiston•Queenston•Lampeter

Library of Congress Cataloging-in-Publication Data

Bunch, Richard Alan, 1945-
    Running for daybreak : poems / Richard Alan Bunch.
       p. cm.
    ISBN 0-7734-3558-1
     I. Title.

  PS3552.U46725R86   2004
  811'.6--dc22

                          2003066482

The Edwin Mellen Press   The Edwin Mellen Press
Box 450   Box 67
Lewiston, New York   Queenston, Ontario
USA 14092-0450   CANADA L0S 1L0

The Edwin Mellen Press, Ltd.
Lampeter, Ceredigion, Wales
UNITED KINGDOM SA48 8LT

Printed in the United States of America

to

the memory of my parents

and to

Rita, Katie, and Ricky

Contents

Grateful acknowledgment is made to the editors of the following publications in which some of these poems, or earlier versions of them, first appeared: *Old Red Kimono, Prairie Winds, Nebo, Hawai'i Review, Studio, Rockhurst Review, Black Moon, Impetus, Caveat Lector, Iconoclast, Coracle, Fire, Kinesis, Mind in Motion, NeoVictorian/Cochlea, Tule Review, MM Review Anthology, Ruah, Cold Mountain Review, Maelstrom, Spindrift, The Plaza, Pinyon, Takahe, Kimera, The New Formalist, Poetry Depth Quarterly, Midwest Poetry Review, Coe Review, Newsletter Inago, Gryphon, Sierra Nevada College Review, Candelabrum Poetry Magazine, Red River Review, New Thought Journal, Snakeskin Anthology, Burning Cloud Review, Paper Salad Poetry Review, Konfluence, Orphic Lute, Ginger Hill, Sonoma Mandala, Lucid Stone, Albatross, Syncopated City, Artemis, Thorny Locust, Wiseblood, Comstock Review, Green's Magazine, Tucumcari Literary Review, Journal of Contemporary Anglo-Scandinavian Poetry, Slant, Oregon Review, Lucid Moon, New Mirage Quarterly, Japanophile, Roanoke Review, Dry Bones Anthology 2000, Twilight Ending, The Alembic, Pinehurst Journal, The Gathering, Concrete Wolf, Green Fuse, Beyond Doggerel, Heliotrope, Dan River Anthology, The Listening Eye, Alternative Arts and Literature Magazine, Brownstone Review, Chaffin Journal, Mid-America Poetry Review, Porcupine Literary Arts Magazine, American Poets and Poetry, Mandrake Poetry Review, The Quest, Axe Factory Review, Fugue, Blue Heron Quarterly Journal of Haiku and Zen Poetry, Poetry Nottingham, Pudding House Publications Anthology, Chaminade Literary Review* and *Sulphur River Literary Review.*

I would like to acknowledge the continued encouragement, assistance, and inspiration of my wife, Rita. Her support through the years is deeply appreciated. I would also like to acknowledge Jim Herrman, my friend since childhood, who has always encouraged my writing even in the early days when publishing a book of poetry was at best a remote possibility. Finally, I would like to acknowledge the help of Patricia Schultz of Mellen Poetry Press in the preparation and support of this manuscript.

"I consider Richard Bunch's poems to be of the highest quality because of their diamond-like beauty...(T)he poems shine yet have a polish and finish...One feels that in reading his poems no changes would be possible, that the language is sharp and incisive, almost like haiku that have been expanded to much longer poems."

—Gary Silva, Professor of English,
Napa Valley College

Of *Summer Hawk*:
"In each poem (Bunch) renders his subject with a zen-like precision which, together with a soft, surreal imagery, give his poems startlingly delightful effects...This (book) is a finely crafted work with a delicate beauty, a quiet melancholy, and a strong individual voice."

—Thomas Wiloch, *Small Press Review*

"(Bunch's) poems strike a sharp tone, as a jazz image. He speaks of the urban, rural, and eternal malaise; and joy of man."

—*Vanderbilt Divinity Review*

RUNNING FOR DAYBREAK

Mozart by the Sea

With green vision she attends to Mozart's
Eine Kleine Nachtmusik, that dark art,
And feels it woven with fresh-fathered seas,
Breathes its beats as her heart bears repeating.
A whole note's but a quarter of her past—
This keeps her married to the summer grass.
She recalls how rhythm can ripen, compose
To apocalypse and how Mozart flows
As natural as breakers breaking to
Sunrise with a looking-glass. In this mood
She beholds a blue sensuousness, a
Cascade of sound, seas that season both ways
Sound keeps feeding, reflects, and weighs her soul
And makes listening fields, the world's blood, show.

Dictionary of Wars

Our veins drown in autobiography,
that resumé of reversals, nuclear
mushrooms, odors of transient flakes.
They gun with smoke the carnage
of misjudgment, chronicled waste.

*

Some avatars specialize
in death by the numbers:
miniature caesars who try
double-crossing kingdoms
of the die through genetics
and genocide.

"The moon's my mother," they all
lie, "the sun's my twin
with legions to prove it."
And those legions are ready
to be fleeced again.

*

Ponder the Crimean War
or maybe the Jugurthine.
Or a campaign as real,
the wars of philosophy:
a spider's phenomenal web,
the world, spun out of the One,
and how that one finally
finds itself in the twittering
of swallows, the timbre and
tune of the mother tongue.

Hunters emerge from the wood
stalking the inflated self.
They know beatific deer
from an emperor of hunger.

Nor are they surprised
at the ascent of buddhas
blossomed above tidal remains
of their former selves.
Amazing what you catch
when you journey
down, down, down, down
where the sun sleeps and

slips.

*

Tail in her mouth
a serpent forms a perfect O,
that yoni circle, the
unbroken we leave broken.
Dreams burning for skylight
thus rise to erect and
struggle to co-direct all these:
the waking of sunless
seas; cutthroats with copper looks
who bandit power for power's shrieks,
and philosophy's intimate mountains,
monologues no less that matter
long after the ends
of the ending earth.

*

Not just seal pups clubbed senseless,
their burgundy blood spilled on spikes
of ice. Nor the condor soaring into a
shadow of itself. Nor barnacled whales
that spew out their short and sad
narratives. Not just these
but earth itself. And the very air.

Few holy ones are breathing here.

*

Thrown. And thrown again. As though fired
into this world we arrive in
funereal cars and
throughout this fleshy
night are marked to be
veins of a tolling vine.
Still we are lured by another shore
to become breakers
of this midnight sun
and thus discern
the sacred
among the murderous weeds.

*

No apparent future? History's sutures
undone? Strained absences and passages—
another turn at the gun.

Dangling

At the mercy of the wood warp
Of indecision, between the famine
Within and a compass without range,
I still dance in a sea penciled with despair
For I have learned to float
By not always trying to fly
With every dandelion self that gusts.

In this field of tenderness
Like some classic gesture, I catch the moon
At its crossing and wait
For a tide steeped with the naming
Of ecstasy.

Mellow Beyond Recall

These islands they green by the sea
For they are lovers at the dawn of
The gods. They reach deeper than
Waking pain. These are the mothers
Of bones, inventors of the final strophe.

These islands, august lovers of a
Friendship of the sun, all marry into the stars.
They do not martyr the details of forgotten
Springs but trace past the wrecks deep down
Through the resurgent maps of bloom.
Mellow beyond recall, they
Enter the blues
Of the sea with its leviathan names.

The mind that sings the green of the sea, the
Dancers whose profiles are the shapers of time,
Are lovers. They are the ones who dream
The dream of endless duplication, who break into
Nakedness for a shore without motion. Nor
Do they reek of fish bones breaking into the sun.

Mellow beyond recall, these islands hide
Desire behind the sex of politics, the politics
Of appearances, the theater that is evergreen.
"Only in one world," they chant,
"Are we one. And nothing less."

Viva le symbolisme. These lovers salvage the body
Where nothing yelps loudest in susceptible love.
We forget and in the bas-relief of our forgettings
Have to repeat our unremembered cargoes
Of pain. In remembrance springs redemption.

Mellow beyond recall, these islands color
All as light, when ignorance is torn from this family
In the blood, a rainbow's rebirth, the primordial *fa*,
The face aflame, purer
Than any blank eye, in the last say of the rose.

The mind that conjures the green of the sea
And its gargantuan crosses of mourning, is a lover
Who in compassion lays the yawn of quivering eyes
On reflection's glass and beholds in luminous sheaths
A lotus, serene voice of the pleromic man.

Four Haiku

among yellow stamens
and this salmon sunset—
a swan's head

*

cloud-wisped afternoon sky
a wild gander skimming waves
takes flight

*

blue jays filled with sunlight
silent now
the peace of lilies

*

kite floating over the beach
people disappear
in yellow fog

Fog

A way of finding yourself
where lost fog clings. Veins of
remembered playlight begin to blur.

Steady heart, wave battalions
pound and blast. You cannot see
them, only savor a restlessness
that whomps as April's blood.

Who you are erases here like a native
earth present in unseen praise.
Masks of rock jut out beyond
the sea and brooding.

Like the you
you once thought you were
they appear to accept this orchestration,
a reminder that fogscapes
are the mind's deadly poem, those
questioning streets
borne in difference.

Two Stones in One Sun

What would we do
sans fire's stream
and water's sand?

no sun makes snow run
no silence swallows sound
no man yields woman
no god finds human ground

sun and moons
resign their turrets of jade…

it finally takes
a you and a me
to fell the bifocal tree
and dip blue guitars
in the earthiest of moons

Three Epigrams

Whoever you're screwing
Could be your undoing.

Could it be the black of your ivory hands
Is the ebony of your pearl's demands?

Is love a tomb with breath's unease
Which death may cure when time doth please?

Rainbows

       Unbutton these precedents, yellow,
and peel back capsuled pastures

       where
blue liquid sky reaches no limit.

We voice suburbs of orange, reflections
       terraced a deeper red.

Green's the innocence that forks
       in passing.

standing with you

in the grammar of death
where burning
mothers unending desire

where sanded cliffs
vie to bluff
the solvent sea's resolve

where the mortar of centuries
knees the dust
and then dissolves

as wild crying dunes howl
spume-spray groundless blows
past the masonry of island names

still the sea the sea the sea
rises to reach
the deepening moon

and with unerring
unsteered intuition
pauses its ancient menacing

allows loves to follow love
that utterly speaks from stones
and anchors unanchored time

Sonoma Mountain

Lying on the couch barely
conscious, my memories slip
and keep slipping
back to the top
of Sonoma Mountain.

Innocence! Shooting metaphors!
Picking wildflowers
firm in their yellowy wisdoms.
Clutching them
with such runaway
tenderness as though
we could undo dying and death.

And your hushed eyes in their philosophic bones
kept asking, borne
with a kind of rage and
outstretched wonder,
how many springtimes
you had left.

Until we wound
back down the trail
and mingled with those maybes once again
no answer arose.

A ranger said we could not
keepsake the flowers.
So we tossed them like chips
high into the flames
and higher still into the riddles
of this twilight.

Night Sweats

Your touch explodes me.
How can I forget bluebells
in bloom, those
cups swollen, and no less the
sweet summer grass?

A pulse this fragile, this volcanic,
takes the tyranny of dust
by the throat.

At the Home for Veterans

Stonehenge still,
in the likenesses of no other love, the veterans

grappling with
the mold of their age, doze. One sleeps in

a wheelchair wrapped
in a plastic tube that snakes

and spans a fitful neck around which hangs
the *Croix de Paix.* Another leans

forward as though she's posed or
poised to hear someone rave orders from
tomorrow's field that was once

a touching past completely out of bloodless martial
hearing.

Still another's cane
rests against his inner seam. A tube huddles around

the tag that names him, a parenthesis
that argues into a void. His dreams no longer seem

to complete the art of war—

now he marshals the sun's missiles into his eye.

                    Just then a coin
plunks down the vending machine's rust-free throat.

Someone in white
                    with a loyalist hand

removes one Dr. Pepper. As they slumber with a foreign
war's sound, the TV

                    fractures
intensities of their snores, dances its war games

                    just this side
of human darkness.

The Perfume and Makeup Counter

Lines form wishes around these mirrors.

*

Giggling girls vie for a scent that lingers.
They pour *L'Eau d'Immortalité* between
Their palms to reproduce a lure for feeling.

*

Once he trims his beard, the former clown
Prefers to be made-up. He does not mind rose water
So he can clown around without false nails.

*

A realtor pries her mid-life out of escrow
And, reading between the breeding lines,
Tries to relive the luster.

*

An older woman, well-dreamed
With bluish hints to her hair
Rubs her wrists together to sample some *Youth Dew.*

*

Mirrors turn by a wish of the wrist.

*

Many try *Opium* at least once.
Or splash on *Eternity.* Usually there are
Shadows still brooding about the eyes.

*

What counts is the drawing back, the
Embrace, wrinkle-steep or not,
Of wear, an obsession
Whose age simply survives.

To Savor

wine, slowly swallow. Savor breezes yellow
in shoulder-high mustard and in
fields where summers rise.

Savor the courage of one who outlasts
the sluggish times of average tyranny.

Savor each moon that rises blue
through the bodies of woodland pines.

Through the slow drip of winter
foretaste once again new wine feelings.

Know too there are rhythms that elope
and savor laurels filled with sunlight
in this streamlined waste of hurry and bury.

Brief Bios

1.

Mary lived to bury her sisters and died
bite by bite by the sheer loss of earth.

2.

In silver wheels Farnsworth rolled
until his soul cost more than his millions.

3.

When rats ate his paper windows, Odie felt
his bludgeoned soul decry the pain of poverty.

4.

At ninety-eight, Elizabeth the bread maker
had broken her share. Pundits applauded.

5.

Cradling the sky, Horace put his thumb
through a dipper of stars.

Rain

We surrendered
through our cravings, embraced

furies in those philosophic limbs.
Our days somersaulted in the wind

bonding with the invisible.
There were wrinkling horizons, way back

then weighty in the April solitude.
And burgundy sunsets

grave with a future's dreams,
nights dancing through each lotus kiss.

That kingdom then unwound, long in passion's teeth,
summoned again in the earned wisdom of rain.

Pressure

Time pressing
the color of blood.

You want to scream
and arm again.

But that won't do.
You know better.

It's like leaving.
You don't want to leave either.

Leaving is not
a solution.

Nor drink.
A false dilemma.

You find another choice
and begin to cherish.

Even this minute
might shape your dreaming,

enflesh your passing wisdoms,
those enchanters by the barn.

Sailing

Sails skirt on glass
as the mind's timbre yields syncopation.

Easterly winds carry
the flesh into unmeasured scales.

Still pitch resumes
skilled at love's canvases and wakes

while the mind's textured reach
(without the shadows of jaws)

sails bluer waters that tint
deeper than mendicants do
with unconscious direction.

The Native Returns

After so many winters, the summer's
Sun swims these worn hands and brightens the wine-
Shouldered hills. Coming home, no more going
Far, far away, I bring these memories
To a living end, one to remember.

A horseshoe tops the door of knotty pine,
Still exiles fortune's shade. Yet home's steep climb
From the past presents some memoried signs:
Eucalyptus odors, moss-ancient oak—
Once these were lost. Now nostalgia's sired
Eyes find poppies on a hill's leafy bed.

Such roots consume me, for they are love's yoke
Where all's remembered as strangeness desired.
After so many winters, winter's dead.

Veins

That leaf is
worth your study on a star-pocked
night beneath
limbs
whose veins shoot
through unscaled sight.

Through them
you summon up your lives
floating through to a summer's deep.

Some, bathed in outer dusk, crisscross
skies
as though surnames perforated
in blood, a milky talc,
puff of nothing.

Each branches
to make a past, crossing
over in a present that unfolds
vibrations of blue.

A Circle of One

It flows where apples ripen.
Along the way rocks
Dissolve mirrors of snow.
It becomes a true cast
Of black spaces, dominions
That wake to lost friends,
Goodness betrayed over tomatoes.

It delights in tidepools
Where starfish stick,
Holds the hearse's wake
In a forever called the sea.
It caresses unwashed
Silences, love does, and tracks the
Center of the sun
In the furniture of each dark music.

When a Colt Pauses at the Spring

In those slick, brooding waters
Skies sail with a primordial silence.

The spotted colt begins to drink and pulls back,
Startled by your veteran loneliness.

Once again he drinks then pauses,
His wondrous eyes opened wider.

He cannot fathom those unfathomed pools
Whether it be in the dress of centuries

Or that dark unmindful mind
Where still he embraces the illusion

That thirst only gathers with age
Or pants for a summer's field of wisdom.

First Fish

Circular to the last, you can retrieve the first.
Imagine lips parted as though to resort to chemistry

As you troll a virgin river without end.
The lines at first seem endless. Then other tests

At twenty, fifty, and eighty, each of them new catches
On each line. Matters soon taste all-too-human, assume

A visible diction—bass, pike, sunfish—shades of an ancient name.
Imperceptibly it becomes harder to snag that first one.

You can retrieve simplicity, the way your first hook,
Hallowed by the everyday, is struck with new luster.

Imagine trolling the river of those departed. How tunnels
At both ends light, hook of that eye first opening.

The Uprooted Baskets at Ridgeview Junior High

(for Jim Herrman)

Mais où sont les neiges d'antan?
-François Villon

Saturday mornings those mouth-shaped hoops
would be there, overnight, still, open
to hold the air as though to suspend us.
Our bikes were parked like a private
audience, a source of solitudinous cheers.

First warm-ups: jumpers, sky hooks,
butterflies in slow motion. Soon we'd
get our "eye," take sides and strides
in sync, a half-court show. Fakes,
dribbles, pivots, dunks: the swishing end
always the same:
                    pure ice cream.

But those plays are gone. Perhaps
we had outgrown that stage. Only gray
patches remain, skeletons of another season,
containing moves only now to be imagined.

Miscarriage

Over your lips
tears
began as the sound of waves
tried over and over
and around to form again
a picture of no one.
No one at home. Or maybe just
maybe hiding.

The womb suddenly
lonely and stark
complete with a walnut-sized
still life, a journey without
a beat.

Sadness shredded those
corners of longing
with deadening silence.

All we could do was hold
on and bear the ticking
loss ever ticking
beneath yellowing roots,
a death as close as no one.

Spiders

Daughters
of night, they spin, weave,
snip destinies of silk.

Each strand the lot
for some suspecting morsel
which crawls or slides or stumbles
into this fellowship of hunger.

Those arms seem so weak,
but hold up the gun and the gun's knife,
accent the perishing, and blind
those who yearn to leave
this company of the gods.

These sisters live
to weave, to span the destined lines.

Someday they might
just stitch this loved earth,
this body's bride, into
winter roses made of silk.

Meditation at Muir Beach

Dunes in miniature wrinkle
the beach's lip as steady winds
whip the sand into beige
ribbed brows.

Whitecaps flare in rhythm;
surf tumbles into galloping
piano fingers.

A lonely gull tames her shyness;
her head tilts inquisitively
as she searches the beach.

Hers is a hunger.

Mine is how to stitch scar tissue,
another crackling of the heart,
one of love's crueler days.

Out there a hospital ship
drones seaward, its funnels
eclipse into fog. It can't
do a thing about these
drops that slowly wind
their way down my body
and color the sand redwine.

But there is in these wild waves
a peace between memories.
I can forget. I have before;
once memory and regret have
buried me in two.

After awhile the bleeding stops
as do the calls, and
like the gull, I shall fly
down the beach
and roll back out to sea.

Cheekin' It

Let's go, let's cheek it
and just go
leave it
and fly
as wild geese fly
with our jeans on
(we've been penned too long)

grab your sea
by the wheels
the sun through
your mind
and let's cheek it

past pink clouds
of New Mexico
and beneath
the southern palm

let's go, let's outa here
and just go

no waiting around
to pay the bills
hanging around
to lease the day
let's swim through sand
past the farthest star
and catch a zebra
by the twilight thigh

let's just cheek it
and eat wild berries on
olde summer roads
and ski dark
winter swans down
until stars
swallow the moon

let's cheek it
drop it all and go
sail the next wave
bravely leaping seawind
and soulward into spring

let's cheek it
leave the worries
the dyings
at home in a jar
and do it,
then scout
beneath a star's hymn
arteries of fire,
and revel in praise
the sun's sacred rise

Mates

Death's opening moves are classic.
Always he takes your horse.

The Queen is not much help. She
Takes cocaine and rocks
Her flesh to sleep.

The King also tries to be an escape artist,
His castle of balloons.

A winter's orchestra,
Death's hand hears knights ahead
Of the bishop's mirth.

There's a pallbearer in love's snow.
Angels rest adrift. And death
Smiles into the next century.

The King keeps running in his tennis
Whites and hides in his castled self.
He confesses he is thinner than the
Hiss of desire, the pianos of night.

Death coughs, under the weather.
He too is persistent. And perishes
In the artful possibility
That you may not exist.

The Homeless

In America.
With walls and without.

Cardboard; plastic capes
to keep the stares buzzing off.

A park bench, grove of heating
pipes they dwell, steam rises on

the most public of our private selves.

City lights blink: they awaken
as pigeons feed, blanket rolls

harden when grounds become colder
than hearts.

They become amusements, freakish
carousels with cigar store Indian

riders, for passengers who do
not want to explore personal

biography and have their veils of
illusion rent.

But they are human, you and I,
us and us, different circumstances,

exchangeable clothes. Humans more
touching than words.

Santa Rosa Plums

My father's ardor, the grafting art,
that budding genealogy of God's delight.
The loving pear's archetypal music,
apple's thoughtless geography,
the wild plum's wilder loins,
a family pigmented with longing.

He stood there in a gray sweatshirt,
old khaki pants, shoes full
of holes, and cut off a pair of
limbs to make a new one.

Then he sliced further down
that soul's anatomy, pried it
open for a virginal smile,
a newer shoot, the Santa Rosa
plum, the ones that redden
deeper with each passing summer's skin.

Strips of bedsheets held
the shoots together. Daubing hot pitch,
he watched as these strange new lovers
dried a dripping
black. Once cooled, he relit his pipe,
grinned, and moved the ladder closer to heaven.

His ardor was hard to resist. In fusion,
he knew, scars were never certain.
They could cleave like politics.

A Sheep's Remains at Fort Ross

The surprise of it could not be
forgotten: balls of wool still attached
to the leg joints and rib cage
which looked as though
it had been crushed at one end.

Buzzards and hawks had picked
those bones into a gray stare.
The wind, constant, relentless
as the steady sea roar a hundred
or so meters away, dried the cage,
ravished its decaying scent and
hollowed out even the skeletal neck.

Sprouting between each rib
and beneath sockets
where eyes once gazed
were tiny yellow flowers
on this headland so windy
only grass and miniature ferns
hugged the earth as close.

Late Summer, Russian River

Endless
  the desire
to halt the hum
  and buzz
and buzz
  of passage
and clutch
  what bubbles
from the restless heart.
  The blood

no longer curious
  flows
long into shadows
  to learn
a latitude of ripeness.
  Still

there is this yearning
  which juts
past the mellowed
  senses, past beauty,
to master fire,
  to season
the discerning eye
  for twilight.

Late summer survives
   when our
shadows engender praise
   at dusk.
Even now in this west wind
   with desire
pulsing with currents
   this yearning
is there, to climb
   down into
the root of stillness
   and touch
her holy skin.

Islands of Indifference
[a picture postcard]

Lasciate ogni speranza
voi ch'entrate.
-Dante

Here words have their edges
sanded smooth so they mesh
with their opposites without effort.
Evil and good run as rivers of uncaring.

Hedonism—lush, tropical, naïve—is
their only god.

Their bodies lie
on beaches like sex objects,
garbage picked clean by
loveless buzzards.

And still there is the desire,
that native conatus, to pass on
forever in the sand.

Easy for them to whisper love
in moments and mean
nothing.
Landscapes here ape mere hunks
of well-hung meat
not as one might be, but mere
chemical convenience, gargoyles
in the flesh, surveyed by the latest
art of the state's technology.

Easy it is to defeat them;
their arms bend like willows.

Some never feel below the surface.
They abort
on the tongue's premeditation.
Others finally reach
their "other Eden."

Here they grows wings
and take another chance
to sharpen their teeth
on one another.

Match on Water

In fact we are lovers. You can tell
by that delicate fidelity
lining the eyes. How we hate
when staying moments go
but remain
captured and captivated
by last gasps
of the stealing sun
coloring through layered clouds
thin as venetian blinds.

Awe and silence
make sacred this setting.
We pull warmth around us
like a circle, a sacrament
of touch, of fragile space
unbroken
by that jagged brow of breakers
come to gnaw the world.

And, too, our eyes are bridgeable
shores of the soul's country,
our hearts rising serenely
into the body's heat, its
passion's philosophy,
its awakened aftertaste.

And the sun? In seconds
it folds into gold and older gold
and with a final swoon
slips
slowly   slowly   slowly
into a bare squint
brightening, o brightening
at the last
rites and bursts
into a match on water.

Seawind in the Plums

This evening
ruffles of surf
draw out shrinking sand.

Casts of the sea pull us.

Holding you here
the rustle of your dress,
seawind in the plums,
the moon's cupped light.

We touch
what a wave marks:
that small world
flared up like split bone.

The sound
resounding of surf
opens us
far beyond
that glib theater of the brain.

Hypnotic sea-veins,
emerald fists,
pull and pull
until we fast become
the underside
beauty between us.

Evening Star

You brighten the red setting sea, break down
Toxins, those ice hearts, spider-clockworms, myth-
Shorn skeletons of unmeaning, unsound
Moons with robot hands,
                    rootless kin and kith.
No plastic fragments, you and I, but more
Than mechanical specimens, or mere
Tools, but hallowed with a human core,
Children alive, willows dancing the earth.

Let's relive the dream of that reverend
Future, where fog-lovers find starry nights,
And whole worlds pulsing alive know no end,
When imagination passes organic heights.

Venus, can you, alone, torch up this rust
Lest our outcast parts mushroom into dust.

Turbulence

Your bottle gleams half-
full as our captain comes
on and tells us what we are
already experiencing
this time over the badlands of New Mexico.

Through the window
mountain wrinkles are still half-
revealed by mirages.
Those are your favorites, mi alma,
something we can agree on.

My favorites are white cloud
puffs that hang suspended like gunshot
and spread their shadows over
a bluff's shoulder.

Still there are winds at cross-purposes here
no matter
why the flight
or destiny of origin.

Tension makes flight memorable,
you observe, in this ritual mating
as another mirage is spotted.

We cannot and do not elude the stress
but zigzag our way
through a canyon of clouds
as we steady ourselves
for the foregone
perception of a flight
filled at the last to half-empty.

Sunset, Kona Coast

for Rita

To the south massive layers of clouds
form island mirages.
Below, lava rocks porous black
once liquid orange flame
vent Pele's volcanic dances, hissing
sulfur, ashen lunar tides,
withstand erupting turquoise surf,
dervishes of spindrift.

This setting's redorange yolk-like sun,
penciled with cloud-gray veins,
breaches that moment
when it rests lightly
on the sea
as though embracing for the first time.

We know work alone sets our suns,
snuffs out
explorations of rainbow solitudes,
eclipses the daring art.

Here we taste time
stopped, live beyond these bodies
in the way love frees, in new birds at dawn,
conversations of raindrops,
cups cracked,
plates with prints color-faded,
in the rhythmic rubbings of palm fronds.

The Edge

You have to be keenly aware
of the axe which smells
of fur and blood.
You have deluded yourself
into thinking
they won't get rid of you
that you have worked so hard and so well
that nothing like this could happen
to you.

And then one fine day (or night
if they're especially nasty)
you discover we all dangle
in separate skins.
Older blood divorces.
Edges of cordiality
suddenly fold
into stone.
Some friends turn out to be
stillborn after all.

You cringe as you hear the good news.
First your titles, your keys,
next your name, your face,
what little urn of space you occupied,
your worth in money and performance
gone.

You think you've become a dismembered dog
with no opportunity.

It's then you realize the vast ocean
of the toilet
you've been treading
all these years.

Then it is time for Zen. You remember
the story. Chased by a ravenous tiger
who aches to eat him,
a man finds himself
hanging over a cliff by two vines
being eaten by three mice.
Below, starved lions
wait to devour him.

While hanging, he sees
a wild strawberry. He plucks
and eats it. And it is
so delicious.

Painted Desert

sunsets aflame
dance
fiercest orange
yielding red
fists of clay

Indian brushes
blush
crimson
thunderstorms
paint
when rain
hammers
those
petaled arms

juniper,
bullsnakes,
wind-scarped
hills: these
faces too
fold
into silence

Composition

You get masked by the lines sometimes
like bluish dye, in the shape of
a wolf's rib, shot through frost
or that other tigress, fire, though
you leave a licking trace
in the foaming measures of afterglow.

And yet at the center of this
where soliloquies intersect
and thread on, the igniting
moment, the unmasked abode, where
we're finally dead and being born.
This is what weds us
long after returning to the basics
of color, to fashioning newer
flutes for the longest descent,
and to the philosophic season
with its hammered truths, trans-
parent deaths, and beauty's
shoulders of corduroy.

Transubstantiation in Blue

yes as lovers we flow
to the sounding sea
poundings the sea hallows
the ever sun-brided sea
you rising out of the me
of me you pine for
in the sunshivering sea
the elements you pine for
in the sea of me

we lovers school the sea
flushed with rebirth
communing loins like
plucked ganders of foam
you can rise from the illusion
of me like mendicants burning
to deep kiss the holy noon

we lovers go to
the resounding sea
in a schooner of souls
herding past history's
fume and rack
and again you rise
out of the sea of me
with no illusions
of fireless eyes
or the politics of hollow eyes

we lovers school the sea
in threshed enskyment
in madness and sad guitars
in summits of unshouldered beauty
in drums of brokered eyelids
connoisseurs of sunslips and slapsilver
we lovers school the sea

Gulls at Jenner

Where the Russian River
rejoins the sea

a way back from that sea
strand's spume-plashed rocks
with nosy harbor seals

a wind-quiet ritual
of land bunches them into

a surrealscape
where memory
caws just long enough to eat

where clay-blue time flattens
into the jaded cargo
of mere being

where listening dunes
shade a forked sun
that nestles ankle-deep
into the suddenness of sand

this lightens their sacred space

Symbolic Straw

In sex and in war
winter comes on dark.

Take that man floating
silent
as though dead
on currents which scarcely move
the moving river.

Birds hunger in the limbs overhead:
nervously they watch him.
They keep waiting
for a thumb to twitch
or a nerve to unnerve.

So far, all they know
is eating
as a form of war.

South by Southwest

Our eyes met each other's reflections
through the arrivals window
at Love Field

> now you say *don't ever leave*
> *don't go away*

But you know how things began
midnight between us
with no ties that bind, no ties at all

> still you say *never leave me*
> *don't fly away*

But you've known all along how
snow fills winter with footprints
and the wind blows them away, away

Through Aging Eyes

How light curves about
Her arms and dying suns
Thread her eyes in
Twilight to close a rose.
Through snowfalls and trees
Creaking heavy above
White-whiskered avenues
She awaits by the fire
Summer's calm to attract her light.

Her noons unfold and crease her chin.
She waters long roses swaying beneath
Graying squirrels
Playing elm to elm. Even westerns
On Saturdays at that lonely
Movie house where each feature
Starts to end
Before it means to begin,
Are prayer wheels held fiercest
To the breast.

Each stroke of her brush adds
Character to her eyes and
Amorous arms on windblown sheets
Each sun a yearning to rise. Her skin colors
A sonata tone, her miracle a
Finite noon,
Her beauty remains uncharted
In chiseled stone.

Necessary Guides

There is a guide to a life
where pleasure means more
than fame. It speaks of a voyage
through a country planted in many generations.

It is at times a seismic
return, that inner ear, prehistoric,
a sutra of secrets where
cherry blossoms always are about to fall.

Yet fame too has its
lingering times. Sometimes it is here,
at others, scopes an alternate universe.
Sometimes it just devours your own hands,
assumes a darkening ecstasy, and
ignores your cultivated ignorance.

The Dancers

There are dancers in pink sheets of water
who cleave the leaves of air
they play the true flute
and crave the rib-root
of the moon's dark daughter's heir.

There are dancers in jade lakes of midnight
who flow to sea in a sigh
where green goddesses walk
and forgetfulness clocks
and dark brides the light of the eye.

There are dancers in blue swans at moonrise
who wag the howls of a hill
and carve out the wind
on a blossom's young chin
until time erases the will.

There's a dancer in dead drums of summer
who hawks the blood-sifting ground
as bone turns the stone
of the everlasting foam
of the one who dances unbound

Sequoia

There were survivors in your family
Too before the kingdoms of Benin and
Ashoka's India, you survived it
All: denying spirit to matter, and
The healing power of rage, captive limbs
Who freed each root's journey, those mother tongues
Of mutual emptiness. Other limbs
Became true heirs for worms. Through fires your lungs
Yet breathed. Circles of seeds became your skins,
Scars of your history, wood of our myth.
You survived when Lao Tzu died praising yin,
The Black Death clenched the dead, genocide blitzed
Us with ash. But before you're axed to jade
Your shorn limbs will hold more than this time's shade.

The Queen Disrobing

Higher than this piano or that castle
Overlooking the Bavarian Alps
Your loves were missed in mist
Like a train not taken to Kyoto or St. Petersburg.
Side by side we conducted
Ourselves so that sky filled with laughter
And mopped up summer's thunder.
We felt mated with amazement.
Baudelaire's uneasy spleen
Could still play and draw out our best. But

After intermission we skated as sun to moon.
Respect's ashen hags tilted, flew away in protest.

All we held in common reverted to each alone.

Baudelaire even dressed as satan's boy
You despairing states of his mistress, I
Admiring his infernal flute, that
Classic of the city. Now you pouted
And sat on opposites sides of the room.
Glowerings, pawings, and whinings
Made us finally converts
To the estrangement of choice.

Essays in Divinity

Cherish in yourself
the birth of God.
       -Meister Eckhart

What is divinity if it can come
only in silent shadows and in dreams?
       -Wallace Stevens

My last poem lying in the dark;
the nurse has left.

I feel my heavy breathing
my chest covered with whiter hair.

Upon me has fallen the hermeneutic
wonder of dreams. In them I dance

like Zorba the Greek and love women
only God's love mystically fashions.

Evenings discover me gazing at lines
etched at the Moulin Rouge by my friend
Lautrec.

In Athens, I discuss particulars of beauty
with Plato who hankers for souls
anchored in stars.

On Lesbos, Sappho takes her girls gently
by the arm and teaches them
poetry deeper than a sigh.

Chaplain motored here this afternoon
espousing Christ and his mystic tide.

She also likes the Buddha's flower sermon
that cuts diamonds made of silk. I would

like to take tea with the lady. She does not
wear her badge like the Pharisees: her

Zen sees too far. Her prayers Om.
There is no room for her love of God.

Dreaming, I see life in other universes
and hear restaurants on the moon within

constellations of light years nearest,
a rainbow's genesis surpassing civilization.

Light stabs as the curtains part. Physician
opens my eyes galloping dream, another pulse!

Dreams have become more real in this last
testament. What we have called reality

becomes a supremely fictive will, Madam.
A door softly opens now:

I hear Neruda in the next age
savoring a breast of his final rose
eternally in flight.

And Tu Fu's brush concentrates
sunsets magenta as plums inspire

each stroke higher than a man: ageless
ways words mother the fathered heart.

Nearness of end: even here dreams
clarify this orange evening

when the sun also rises
in the shape of Mexico.

with the sun no longer

cold
        the Buddha

sat beneath heaven's tree
        and traded

one mortal day
        for a diamond cutter

Fisherman from Calcutta

Once an old man arrived in a village far away.
He heard bickering through the lungs of extremity.

Then he turned to the sun and stared.
He had gone into the sea only to ask:

Why do these lovers get caught
On the addiction to this, the id of that?

He could gaze at the sun for hours
While everyone else learned to panic.

As he kissed the thudding horses of illusion,
He embraced the drums of peace, his undying every breath.

In him was sea, sky, and land, a promised
Dedication to the elusive silence he listened for.

Homing

I celebrate you
God like the innocents

    the beauty
    of lovers.

So many winters
have I flung my sad nets to the sea

    and lost
    even the scent of your name.

Idol of the Tribes

How many angry masks do you bear
In your knapsack of protean names?
Everywhere you appear
And do a reading
There's an outbreak
As though cloned by magic: another power
Stab, a compass for those killing
Fields, genocide eyes,
A current purge of the blood,
Some clutching revelation
Or issue descending.

You and those midnights rising.
You ache in us for we are lovers.
But you grasp those secret advantages
The deuces of this play, its hairline limits.
Just as parabolas come near
But never can quite touch
Infinity, so we flee freedom, from its engaging
Terrors, its atlas of choices.
And when the moon hides
Behind the temptation

Of ancient times, we crawl back,
Chains and all, to you,
Our own *fuegos inclinados,*
Always seeming
So godlike before us,
Reinventing your latest
As our lidless eyes, past
Desperation's blindest need,
Come to terms, readjust
To what is called cave light.

Shapeshiftings

There is something that does not die, the destiny
Of experience. God sometimes disappears.
The world's night is not always holy.

In fact we can at least be double-minded:
The lucretian prelude that may ripen into Don Giovanni,
Pilot molecules on a slope of slippery
Calculation with gas enough to liquidate the
Human and cock the reloaded pelagian guns.

Or where waves née particles prefer
(and cometh now, love, the mystery)
In dancing solitude the beloved
Community, intricate logics of soul,
Butterflies angle in resurrection's motion,
And the unwritten destiny, your original face
Before you were born, first insights invite.

Thomas' Fire

[When a friend urged Thomas Aquinas to complete
his *Summa Theologica*, he said: "I cannot; such things
have been revealed to me that what I have written seems
but straw."]

Treatises heaving with theological questions
which are thorns in the hands of his answers.
His logic explores shapes of the parabola
to conclusions of the premised flesh.
A bell reminds him to put away this bread-breaking
with St. John, Avicenna, and Aristotle.

Something happens
in this death
of afternoon, call it
surprise   of presence
an infinite yes
to stars and soul and sea:
from beyond the beyond
the set of redorange sets
of sun   inward ecstasy
takes him

slowly climbs his spinal energies
through nostrils more revealing

than natural reason's natural high
rolls the flesh into aisles of the sacred

where a rood of roses
ravages heretical with color

and squeezes centuries with pensive petals
where soldiers of intuition glimpse forever

where vision burns uncharted by time
and hell's mensural heart

where stones itch with curious
enclaves of sculpted desire

where the wisdom of God courts a deeper
grammar, the miracle of silence

and mortars of language shape sunlights
unforgettable in the moonshivers of praise

His answer implodes and explodes
wordly if and unworldly then

a high noon
                    the color of sunrise

Degrees of Green at Goat Rock

from here you can watch
waves blaze into

horizons that bleed and stretch
to the sun's mediaeval eye

refining the sleeves of God

where waves whomp
screaming and sunshiver
in a syntax so deafening

they pirouette
in the moment of God dancing

Existenz

Not the whole day. Not even the whole slice.
But a flare, a sun on the cliff, however damp.
One filling of the lungs, in love's
bruised-purple wake, and you can rise
to eat the sun.

That rising is what is missed
when edges are pressed out past
the urinary gold frame;
that larger understanding
can prompt you
to completely miss the blues
in the hands of Renoir's
woman at the piano
so you do not live your heart's summer.

Brokenness is essential,
the shorn limb that maketh whole.

Rivers of the Sea

I watch the ducks and the fishermen too
And the woman who threads by the water.
A dog's tied to the rail of the trailer
She bought way back when her clothes were brand new.

Somehow she survives though not like who's who
In a rich loneliness but through hangers
Loaded with skirts and pants and choice strangers
Along the way. Beer, bread, potatoes, stew—

These bones help firm her blood. The fishermen
Too wait at low tide, their poles pointed straight
Down the river's 3/4 time. They chat low

In pink sails of the wind as a gull tends
The reeds. And the ducks? They mate and await
Greener currents, sometimes yes, sometimes no.

Milton's Muse

I have lost my socks to Milton's muse
And found my tissues in nets of hills
Where sunsets dance in flaming shoes
And burning oak in an ageless well.

I have lost my pants to Milton's muse
And thunder my child in drowsy blood
Where twilight lovers snake in the blues
And mellow within the pulse of drums.

I have lost my ties to Milton's muse
Who rankles time with an inch of leaves
And offers homage to veins of mood
And yanks yogis from the bartered earth.

Notes of a Survivor

How difficult to deny
Those predator appetites
Especially during searching
Flashes of light that erupt between the pines.

We have a rule: don't eat during the day.
After catching a glimpse
Of those cravings on shore we've found
We lose some of our best numbers

That way. Sunset's at both ends of the scale
For these authorities on a disappearing art.
Take my aunt: she went for it.
Poosh! Strung out. And two of my cousins,

They couldn't wait for the dark.
They resisted being
Obscure, without a truer name. Instead,
They leaped for the inviting lights, grave

Appeals of ear and eye, the sensuous razing
Of time. So far, I've strayed past the sign once
To the middle with schools of the others,
Floating counter in clockwise circles

Not to touch the earth or whirl silt
At the bottom or linger
Any longer than it takes to leap
Into the air, a wishbone of faith

And defiance. That way, I've survived
In this farm as one trout who can smell
Leaps ahead and trust the pool
Will not be cast out further up.

Perennials

Roses my friend offers
drip a slow pace.
For you, she says, *a bounty.*

Fragrances of these confederates
light up
for me marines of the dead
where stamens sustain Shiloh
and memory's crosses that endure
stunning white in Flanders' greenest fields.

Outside Auschwitz lilies
mark the blur
of biographies, shoah, indelible red poppies, cinders.

A thin dust floats,
blooms stretch skin above Hiroshima,
eyes, wake by swollen wake, sealed.

In 2020 as if from purgatory in 1945—
A mother and daughter await
a father's return
from another zealotry.
Flowerings suspended by centuries
march in a riot of shells.
Black swans encircle, in baby's breath, continents
that divorce, marriages that outlast
the last.

From the earth, they're for you,
she says,
perennials.

Unveiling

We kiss beneath white wild stars
and open this earthly summer.

For so long I have surrendered
myself to random joys
like a sleepwalker
who fears her darker wisdoms,
her deftly-stitched bounds
between earthbound need
and castblind wish.

No longer.

Your eyes in mine
bloom into attar sloops of wind.

Memories burning with you
will upturn more bliss
than any marriage
in the mouth.

With you I will no longer reminisce
the future and its lidless griefs.

Amenities

Her needles move now by instinct.
Memory's threads over memoried tread.
A patchwork between what is
In the cards
And secondhand gossip
Like the olden days
She still beholds.
Yet whenever her needles pause
As though suspended
There's a curious lethean air.

She remembers how it was
Some years ago out watering
The easter lily and the ash
When she partly unraveled.
Her eyes they dimmed
Only to disclose
A face strangely
Gentled. She remains
In yesterday's mold.

Her children have dropped by since.
And both times, no
Just once, they fought
Over the price of selling her
True estate.

Still she holds to the golden days.
A kind of piece with bygone griefs.

Her fingers are now moved
Not by whether
It rains or clouds, but
By instinct and that alone
Along those threads that thin.

Enchantments

By sheer survival, the moon suggests
the classical, sometimes
being outshone by the range
of choices, and in repeated exposures
grows passive, a deflated stranger
in a mantra of aloneness
though cast always young
to the resurgent core.

Through a magical arithmetic,
a global collage, that
anachronism
called in theory the present,
hauntingly postmodern, nearly comic
(if not ironic) the moon's
texture confesses
(and supposedly empties)
that complexion's reflection
from a text without a context.

But such misses the conception
between fold upon brooding
fold, through interstitial
tissues of rain, sun and
wild wind in season
and out when
the moon still pours

a softer light
into those uncut futures,
the heart shapes
of childhood, a light
older than that sound of oars
dipped by the crew of Ulysses
into open sea, more prehistoric
than art carved on the walls of caves
that engenders vision,
nakedly young, organic.

To Kiss the Earth Again

Untie that mind
reasoned to the death
above thighs of earth's last moon.

Clear the debris
of intimate scalpels
and live the music unconquered.

Untie that body
and let ardor rip
tangs of the smoking sun.

Canoeing

The way she breathes with each deep stroke that feeds
Eddies and swirls, her paddle arches wide
As though to turn. But the currents that breed
The most difficulty are those well-tried,
Need deeper strokes. They're biases that shift
Their histories along the waterline
With scars. She finds it hard now not to drift,
To keep stroking in despair's wake, to find
Cathedrals in waves, genius in turning
Back to where she's come from, sometimes has to
Steer toward the shore, avoid the current's
Mainstream whose sunset cargoes can slice through
Some that are unsung. She knows too how pools
With each stroke change, how currents vie like schools.

Doctor No

Occam's razor de-
constructs the common
thumb, announces coming monsters,
moons with blood spots,
a turtle on its back in late winter's vowels.

Not
to mention lusts of willows, players
spicy with allusions, a genesis
that does not
end with amens
declaiming in unriddled stone.

Who breeds a future of none:

no context
including interstellar histories

no insights
beneath power play currents

no horizons
deeper than paper wounds

no flesh-hewn
psalms uttered truth like that.

Cutting

for C.P. Cavafy

cardboard boxes
in the garage with a coral blade
the fluent sun a mandrake
melting me
to turn again to Colchis

thinking of you Cavafy
on your meanderings to Ithaca
or
poised for releasing

love outside that blowzy cafe
awaiting the spitfire sheets

of Eros
your clothes half-torn
in the grotesque
glare of day
where you embrace
a passion distilled

a politics that remains
unwearied by the Greek sun
unwithered by the Byzantine sky

Dental Visit

Hear that tongue move.
Against the tooth, inside this cheek.
Along these prehistoric molars.

Hissing the air it gives birth:
A little world
Conceived in sound to sound out this one.

A pause between changing saddles
And the vision of God.

Between the country and the city
Roots whisper something
About human fate, dive into time's curved space.

They taste how the tongue glides
When the silence, in a breathless wave,
Still has this much to say.

The Port of San Francisco

A windy, clear day
in the soul of the body's wartime-
gray.

Blown clear of fog,
there spreads a mercy
so unreal
peace and parades
sweeten the hour
of each unbelieving year.

When Music Dreams

Through dreaming seems
Awake to be—
Apples compose your dream.

In times of forget
Listen to remember—
Wild surf in true November.

Seeming grows
To perpetual stills—
Lupines realign the hills.

Dreams dream to remember
Who forget notes that scheme—
Be in the fiesta of seem.

Forget will's forgetting fare
Seems remembers ages—
Hibiscus for your hair.

Grow to wake
Play to seem—
Only petals dare scale the dream.

The Compleat Anglers

after Izaak Walton

Wind claws water
With a simple faith in abiding silence.

Pines circle pines
Whenever a bluegill or rainbow rises.

Ducks search treetops for a skein
Of wild geese in flight

As skies sheep-mellowed on a lost wisdom
Fleck deepening water.

Fish diving underground awaken
The magic hearse.

Water splicing mind carries its master
Down to a purple sea.

Trees scissoring sky
Rip through jaded confessions

While butterflies eluding age
Undress summer beneath a trout-swirled fog.

Winter Sutra

In each lotus a disclosive return.
In each passion an artist on the run.
Peer closely: between flushes of
Unearthly light the holy root quakes.
Birds startle at the moon's path.
Outer skin no longer hawks hunters' aims.
From lakes of vinegar paradise rises.
Beads like these entwine with mystery—
In its unbearable scorching velocity, its
Hearing through the sway of merely eyes,
Its threshold of the frozen—
The mystery that compasses us.

The Winners

for Max Money

No way to win this one, I thought, no way
Since these jocks leaped hurdles faster than I
Had ever done. One's time, 14.5
Seconds, set a record in recorded race
Before I even started. Two stars, they
Brayed how fast they'd go and lose us behind,
Said they'd cheer us from start to finished line.
Into the blocks we set, arms taut, legs spaced,
Spikes shot like smoking tires, comets that shred
Space. At the fourth hurdle both stars crashed and
A third was caught.
                              We took ribbons, hardly won,
But finished our personal lot instead
And found a way to be in such a span
And fashion some stars from what might have been.

Sky Blue

Can you finger that skyey
Riot come of age with frost, mountains
Furrowed, the tympanics of spring?

The hymns, thrums abuzz
With mustard-deep illuminations
Unplucked from April's fields,
And still stroke the central sound,
Tip the primordial wine?

Listen. Explode the now
With a delicious silence
To forge beyond blood-bred twilights,
Bellow past the smoking dragons
Brow-deep, atom-steeped in ideologies.
For the end sky drums the bluest blue.

Poppies Gathering

Green sloped searching hills
splash toward the sea
with its dissolving beaches
and cormorants diving.

In mustard fields, out of
darker spaces, these tongues
exhale sunlit
flame orange to breezes.

Beneath theologies
blue shadows interlace the journey—
behold: this lingering fruit
the lovers almost.

Healdsburg

Midpoint October. Layers of leaves
careen into summer's passage.
Last blazes shiver on
the Russian River.

Winds still purge as they did in July
and from the falls voices rise
sounding motion within the rock.

No one wants to go home. Not even
the fishermen and children
popping balloons.

On the bridge cars chase
reflections bouncing off waves.
Further down river, its whistle belting,
a freight with a cargo of timber
pauses to couple
awaiting the signal *heave*.

Oars dip silently
as two kayaks
slice
through the bluegreen water.

Along a slope of sand
a dog breaks into a fresh run.
All the while
summer still tugs.

Confetti-light leaves shimmering
by the falls
reflect
the motionless eye
of a dozen blackbirds
peerless, autumnless,
resting like charcoal buttons
on a seasoned transmission line.

The Man Who Never Fit

Easy rounds and compulsive days
      Of soapboxes and TVs
      Were not he.

He tried, yes he tried, he did
      He tried winters there and roots then;
      But he did not fit.

And the fits the townsfolk
      Fitted him for: salesman and bullseye
      Were not he.

The shrink theorized
      And the doctors hypothesized
      But their pictures were not he.

Dying early enough in life
      To starve in profits
      Was not he.

Job on job he tried
      Perhaps a marriage or two would do;
      But it was not he.

A misfit was his theme
      He sang as though stars were poems;
      And no one understood except he.

He explored a kind of love;
      To fit him with none
      Was the way his fit was finally one.

black tiny birds

convolutions, double helixes
        swarms in dark clouds they
fan out amoeba and rifle-
        shaped, photonic
pulsings that march to time with a hundred tulips
        swarming
thickets of black sunlight
        cartwheels of foam
blue horses of snow they
        cleave and leave

        smokecurls of locusts
cheekbones inclining, finger
        flights, hairless footfalls of air these
black bandits swoop
        and saddle
into self-generating
        jelly clouds, worming
and storming scores
        of night
word-boats, hammering
        undulations of black necklaces...

Vermont Suite

Vermont greens
Deeper than redorange
Notes. Deeper still the boiling
Post-glacial springs
Where pools murmur
Vibrant with fugues.
Wintry tree limbs
Contain the psalms of summer
And frost hounds
Despite steeples sunlit.

Soon sleepy sugar maples
Yawn with an unhurried pitch.
Surrounded by dandelions,
A sorrel barn harmonizes
In May's pastoral beds.
Bridges timbred in stained wood pose
Accompanied by congregations of yellow.
Conversations turn in
Awe among levitation purples.
Even rainbows round
To ultraviolet
Where what blooms
Stretches unspoken grace.

The Millennium

Some will gather at the river
Or listen to the gong
And wait for the feast.

Some will look back
At this planet and discern what is still
The pulse of green.

Others will have a chance to erect
An island of undying trees and stars.

Still others will rediscover the one
Ancestral coup
And explore the continents of fault.

A wishbone rises to the surface:
In one direction, indictment for
The voices of terror. In another, a lineage
Of chance for the chords of dialogue. I say

Bring on the reverend mysteries, flavors
Of the magnificent.
Few mysteries have we escaped—
The sun rises, ever rises from the sea.

Learning to Ride

Make sure the girth is tight around the belly.
Hold the stirrup steady.
Put your foot in and swing up and over.
As desire shows, you may act like you have
Mounted a mountain. Hold tight the reins but none too
Tight. Don't let this behemoth swim away.
Stay on as long as those captain feelings allow.
The saddle may slip but hang on and
Into the waves glide away. There are times when
You may think you are drowning. But when resurfacing,
The life of breath, with all its talk of death smiles,
Celebrates as though it were the day after paradise.

Apple Dreams

Apple dreams bloom, seashells that cradle
roar at the losses.

Eyes buried long ago, you've lost
at love before (as have i)
between firesides earth and seaside sky
you sigh, you sigh dare we try
again
although there's summer hays to get lost in
and hide such longings from midsummer
roses, safe, unfound.

But hiding is to die
and not string violins in bone.

Love's best again and poetic—
can *we* roll back the stone?

Apple dreams bloom, seashells that cradle
roar at the unknown.

Six Poems

Cumuli gather like summer swans
As philosophers ache
For what is gone.

*

You undress blue flowers at dawn
And celebrate the times
In time's taut skin.

*

Cathedrals teach in the roar of glass
To breakers that whine
For an hour's mass.

*

You reach within for courage and color
And touch a seascape
Of hereafter's hand.

*

This reception weds two summits as one
To flirtations of sky,
Summers of dark.

*

With its zesty blood, your secret itch
Turns smaller hands
Into a stammered kiss.

Sawing Wood

In uncut wood one way yields
To cut, a message you can deny.

Another angle or degree? To avoid the field
You are and flow with all that be may be.

Should a saw's teeth crook and warp
Your true love molders.

Against the grain, best blades dull
To revel no more.

What intimate finishes you are cry out
Though many saws saw louder than love does.

Yielding Our Bread

Perhaps memory is what yields
Our bread, that taste for those infinite
Apples that do not end
In the fruit of bitter days
Climbing darkly, darkly
Like roots of night
Forgotten by habit
In the overdose of routine.

No, here are clearings
In the unclearings of despair,
The kind of day when one
Can still see sails on a turquoise sea.

That taste of remembrance
Rises and slowly ever rises
Unlike a valley pelted and bleached
Dry with broken bones.

Shadows

Chacun est l'ombre de tous.
                    -Paul Éluard

1.

With you to kill one man is to kill all time's
flesh-sawn waste.

Contemplate that scarred moss-slicked
moonburst evening within

itching to chant *o dark film darkening
become that lightning voice where mountains free the heart.*

2.

With you to compose is to sketch
the first course of the first citizens of chaos

who return, through the deliberate eyelids of
fable, to the returning art.

Pray you, teacher of oblivion, rip open your blood-drawn
blouse and caress the flanks of dawn.

For All the Ducks I've Fed Before

they're always there, feasting,
stroking, pleading, sleeping
sometimes plump, usually quite round

almost too plump for mating

London, Nashville, Valley of the Moon
they're always there, eager
for bread on the waters cast
hens quacking, drakes colorful,
quieter, their orange feet lazily
trailing feathered entourage

primping, diving with wings flashing
or feeding poised with tails pointed
heavenward,
daring you, just daring you
to do something
about their brief exposures

February nights warming
their beaks beneath wings
in down and down

then April's rituals leave
breeding marks on the rear
of the hen's nearly drowned head

they're always there, feeding,
stroking, pleading, sleeping
sometimes plump, usually quite round

Running for Daybreak

Stretched beyond horizons of breath
Those muscles pound into the beach's strand.

The sun unveils breathlessly on water
Like rain-filled willows that branch into spring.

Combing waves mark the shore and sultrier markets—
Sweat beads your shoulders row on thirsting rows.

Ahead, stars await behind a forgotten moon.
Daylight fritters vermilion and poppy on its way south.

As that breathing slows, the pace begins to go.
You need another light to get through this night,

To remember there are ways to be still
In the sometimes nowhere of all this commotion.